venison

I am particularly proud to be associated with Christian and Ingela at Highland Game. Their tireless enthusiasm for marketing a completely wild, top-quality, healthy Scottish product namely Venison, is infectious. Their passion for their product is plain for all to see that meet and deal with their company, and they have deservedly won several prestigious awards. I am only too delighted to create these recipes for such a unique product.

Buying Wild Venison couldn't be easier – lift up the phone or order online and it will be delivered direct to your door. The specially designed packaging is guaranteed to keep the product in prime condition throughout the journey.

Cooking Venison could not be easier. Treat a cut of Venison like a cut of top quality beef, then you can't go wrong - there is no difficulty in cooking Venison. Highland Game Venison is hung for a minimum of time so that it's flavour resembles that of good quality highland beef, but with a richer, almost sweeter taste. It is exactly this sweetness that makes it very popular with children – especially when minced Venison is made into burgers, lasagne or meat sauce for pasta – and it is almost fat-free.

Wild Venison is lean meat with little or no saturated fat, making it a healthier alternative to many cuts of beef. It is also as organic as only a truly wild animal can be.

I find the best way to cook Highland Game Venison is quickly with no fussy ingredients. There are so many beautifully prepared cuts to choose from – from mince and stir-fry strips to racks and fillets.

The secret of cooking really tender and juicy Venison is not to overcook it and to rest the meat for at least 10 minutes before carving or serving – this will work wonders for the texture and flavour. Always cook your Venison until either rare or rosy to ensure maximum flavour and tenderness.

Such a wonderful wild product should be treated with the utmost respect, so follow these recipes specially created by me for Highland Game, and you can't go wrong. I hope you enjoy them and make Venison part of your every day diet, not just for special occasions. I certainly do!

Maxine Clark

Maxine is an award-winning cookery writer, inspired cookery teacher and talented food stylist. She has been cooking for over 25 years, dividing her time between Scotland, London, Italy and France. After working for many years in London she has returned to her native country and lives in beautiful Perthshire, the larder of Scotland.

To my father,

who encouraged me, my brother and sisters to experiment in the kitchen and enjoy the world of food.
Our kitchen was turned into a vibrant food market every Saturday morning when my father would cook for hours whilst dancing and singing.
My father had shelves laden with spices and always had fresh herbs growing in the garden - before it became fashionable.
I am so grateful for growing up in a home where food was the central focus that kept the family together. I learned to appreciate a wide range of produce which my father would blend with love and finesse in every dish, from the simplest to the most complicated recipes.
I hope to pass on my father's passion for food to the next generation and keep cooking healthy, nutritious and tasty food.

Marketing Manager, Highland Game

working together with:

General Cooking Guidelines
All recipes and cooking guidelines in this book are specifically for Red Deer Venison.
Venison is not difficult to cook. Treat Venison as you would a cut of quality beef - then you can't go wrong. The golden rule is not to overcook it. Venison does not contain any fat and overcooking will make it dry and tough.
Venison is best served rosy-pink or rare.
All ovens should be pre-heated to the temperature specified in the recipe. For fan oven temperatures refer to the oven manufacturer's instructions. Cooking times are guidelines only and will depend on individual ovens and personal taste.
All spoon measurements are generous.

Published 2005 by:
Highland Food Group Ltd., Baird Avenue, Dundee, DD2 3TN, Scotland. Tel. +44 1382 827088
British Library Cataloguing in Publication Data. A catalogue record for this book is available from the British Library.
Design, Photographs and Text © Highland Food Group Ltd.
Design by Catch
Photography by Stephen Kearney
ISBN 0-9551036-0-6

contents

venison and cranberry tartlets

Spectacular little tartlets to serve at your drinks party. They are assembled in moments – and everything can be made ahead.

Heat a ridged griddle pan until smoking hot.

Rub the Venison with olive oil and season with salt and freshly ground black pepper.
Sear on the griddle for 2 - 3 minutes then turn the heat down to medium and cook without moving for another 2 - 3 minutes.

Turn over and cook for a further 3 minutes for RARE. Cook for 2 - 3 minutes longer for MEDIUM RARE.
Lift onto a plate, cover loosely with foil and leave to rest for 10 minutes. You can leave this to become completely cold. Slice up as thinly as you can.

Set out the pastry cases on a tray. Spoon a tsp. of cranberry sauce into each case.
Top with a twisted slice of rare Venison. Add a blob of soured cream, a sprinkling of chopped chives and a couple of long chives to garnish.

Grind over some black pepper and serve immediately before they have a chance to soften.

---

serves 6

one 150g Pavé (steak) of Venison

olive oil

12 bought or home-made mini pastry tartlet cases

4 tbsp. cranberry sauce (preferably home-made)

4 tbsp. soured cream or crème fraîche

chopped fresh chives and long chives, to garnish

freshly ground black pepper

seared venison niçoise

A warm Mediterranean salad of Venison - a really good dish for a summer lunch or buffet.

Mix the lemon juice, olive oil, half the garlic, salt and pepper in a non-metallic dish. Add the Pavé of Venison (steaks) and toss to coat in the marinade. Cover and marinate in a cool place for 1 hour.

To make the dressing, whisk the olive oil, wine vinegar, remaining garlic, mustard, capers and chopped mixed herbs together in a small saucepan, and leave to infuse.

Meanwhile, boil the potatoes in salted water for 15 minutes or until tender, adding the beans 4 minutes before the potatoes are ready. Drain the potatoes and beans. Remove the beans to a bowl, slice the potatoes thickly and add to the beans, moistening with a little dressing. Peel and quarter the eggs. Pile the potatoes and beans onto a shallow serving dish.

Heat a ridged griddle pan or heavy skillet until smoking. Remove the Venison from the marinade and pat dry with kitchen paper. Put the Venison on the griddle to sear for 2 - 3 minutes then turn the heat down to medium and griddle without moving for another 2 - 3 minutes. Turn over and cook for a further 3 minutes for RARE. Cook for 2 - 3 minutes longer for MEDIUM RARE. Lift onto a plate, cover loosely with foil and leave to rest for 10 minutes.

Meanwhile, arrange the sliced tomatoes and quartered eggs on top of the potatoes and beans.
Thinly slice the Venison and pile into the centre of the salad. Finally, scatter over the anchovies and olives, heat the remaining dressing until almost boiling and pour over the salad.

Serve immediately whilst still warm with crusty bread and lots of chilled Provençal rosé.

---

serves 4

for the garlic marinade:

2 tbsp. freshly squeezed lemon juice

5 tbsp. olive oil

4 garlic cloves, crushed

two 150g Pavé (steaks) of Venison

for the warm dressing:

6 tbsp. extra virgin olive oil

2 tbsp. wine vinegar or lemon juice

1/2 tsp. Dijon mustard

2 tbsp. capers, rinsed

3 tbsp. chopped mixed herbs such as tarragon, chives, basil, and chervil

350g small waxy potatoes

175g fine French beans

3 soft-boiled eggs

2 large ripe tomatoes, quartered or sliced

one 50g can anchovy fillets in oil, drained

50g black olives

salt and freshly ground black pepper

ingela's venison and apricot terrine

This pretty terrine makes an impressive starter served with a salad of bitter leaves drizzled with a walnut or hazelnut dressing, and is just the thing for a special summer picnic.

Mix the apricots with the brandy, cover and leave to soak for a couple of hours.

Mix together the Venison, pork, fresh ginger, allspice, juniper berries, salt and pepper with the wine or port and the olive oil. Cover and marinate overnight or for as long as you can.

Preheat the oven to 180C/350F/Gas Mark 4. Line a 1 litre terrine or loaf tin with the pancetta or streaky bacon, keeping 3 - 4 rashers for the top.

Beat the egg into the marinated Venison mixture, then use just under half to fill the base of the terrine, pushing a 1.25 cm ridge up all around the sides of the terrine.

Spoon the apricots into the hollow created by the ridge, then carefully cover with the remaining Venison mixture to encase the apricots completely. Smooth over and cover with the rest of the pancetta or bacon, folding over any stray strips.

Cover with foil, place in a bain-marie and bake in the oven for 1 1/2 - 2 hours or until a skewer inserted into the middle, comes out clean.

Remove from the oven and place a weight on top. Cool then chill.
To serve, run a knife around the edge of the tin and turn the terrine out. Serve at room temperature with good crusty rolls or bread, gherkins and pickles, or with a small leafy salad.

---

serves 6

75g chopped dried apricots	6 juniper berries, crushed
3 tbsp. brandy	100ml dry red wine or port
500g minced Venison	2 tbsp. olive oil
350g minced belly of pork	175g thinly sliced Italian pancetta or streaky bacon
1 tsp. fresh ginger, grated	1 egg, beaten
2 allspice berries, crushed	salt and freshly ground black pepper

the home - made monarch burger

Adding a little cream or mayonnaise to the burger mixture will keep the Venison moist. Do not overcook or the burger will become dry.

Heat half the oil in a frying pan and add the onions. Cook until soft and golden brown. Cool. Mix the Venison with the onions, then work in the egg and cream or mayonnaise (optional). Season very well with salt and pepper and mix well until the mixture comes together. Divide into four and, using damp hands, shape into thick patties.

Heat the remaining oil in a frying pan and cook over a medium heat for about 4 minutes on each side for MEDIUM, less if you like them MEDIUM RARE. The burgers should be nice and crunchy on the outside.

Choose your favourite roll or bun, split and toast lightly on the cut sides. Spoon a generous dollop of guacamole onto the base of the bun and cover with sliced ripe tomatoes, top with the cooked burger, a few finely sliced red onions and serve with or without the lid.
Serve with extra fresh dips and relishes on the side. Instead of chips, serve a pile of mixed vegetable crisps.

The Healthy Monarch Burger:
Choose your favourite roll or bun, split and toast lightly on the cut sides. Using a potato peeler, shave long strips from a cucumber and carrot, then marinate them for 5 - 10 minutes in a light French dressing or in Teriyaki marinade. Spoon some tomato salsa onto the base of the bun, top with the cooked burger, add a few baby spinach leaves then top with a pile of cucumber and carrot ribbons. Serve with or without the lid.

Variations:
Cheesy Chilli Burgers - add 1 tsp. mild chilli powder and 75g grated strong cheddar to the basic mixture.
Gherkin and Pickle Burgers - add 2 tbsp. finely chopped gherkins and 2 tbsp. Branston pickle to the basic mixture.
Tomato, Pine Nut and Anchovy Burgers - add 1 tbsp. tomato purée, 1 tbsp. toasted pine nuts and 2 drained chopped anchovy fillets to the basic mixture.

serves 4	4 tbsp. double cream or mayonnaise (optional)
for the burger:	to assemble the burger:
4 tbsp. olive oil	four interesting and delicious rolls or buns
1 medium onion, very finely chopped	guacamole, sliced tomatoes, sliced red onions, dips and
500g minced Venison	relishes
1 small egg, beaten	salt and freshly ground black pepper

venison steak sandwich

This is not just a tough piece of old Venison stuffed into an undercooked baguette – this is very classy stuff indeed, made with incredibly tender Pavé of Venison, marinated then cooked to perfect pinkness, sliced thinly and served in toasted ciabatta with mustard mayonnaise and rocket leaves.

Place the Venison in a plastic bag with the teriyaki marinade and sesame oil and turn to coat the steaks in the marinade. Seal the bag and chill for at least 2 hours, turning occasionally.

Mix the mayonnaise with the mustard and season to taste.

To make the caramelised onions, melt the butter in a frying pan and add the onions. Stir to coat with the butter, add 2 tbsp. water, cover and cook over a gentle heat for 10 minutes. Uncover, sprinkle with the caster sugar and balsamic vinegar and turn up the heat. Cook over a brisk heat for about another 10 minutes, stirring from time to time, but watching it like a hawk! The onions should start to turn a beautiful rich brown colour – if not, just cook a little longer. Set aside when cooked.

Heat a ridged griddle pan until smoking hot. Remove the Venison from the marinade and pat dry with kitchen paper. Put the Venison on the griddle to sear for 2 - 3 minutes then turn the heat down to medium and griddle without moving for another 2 - 3 minutes. Turn over and cook for a further 3 minutes for RARE. Cook for 2 - 3 minutes longer for MEDIUM RARE. Lift onto a plate, cover loosely with foil and leave to rest for 10 minutes.

Lightly brush the ciabatta loaf with olive oil then toast on the griddle or under the grill. Slice the Venison thinly.

Spread the bases of the toasted ciabatta liberally with mustard mayonnaise, top with salad, then with the Venison, then the onions, more mayonnaise and finally the ciabatta tops. Cut the loaves in two or four and serve immediately.

---

serves 4

two 150g Pavé (steaks) of Venison	2 large onions, finely sliced
2 tbsp. teriyaki marinade	2 tsp. caster sugar
1 tbsp. sesame oil	1 tbsp. balsamic vinegar
6 tbsp. mayonnaise	2 ciabatta loaves, split in half
2 tbsp. wholegrain mustard	75g fresh rocket or young salad leaves
50g unsalted butter or olive oil	salt and freshly ground black pepper

venison spaghetti sauce

Venison makes a rich and delicious sauce for pasta – particularly spaghetti. It contains little or no fat, except for the added olive oil. This is a particular favourite with children. Make a large batch and freeze in individual portions so that you always have a quick meal to hand.

Heat the olive oil in a saucepan, add the pancetta or bacon, and cook over a medium heat for 2 - 3 minutes until just browning. Add the onion, carrot, and celery, and cook for 5 minutes until beginning to brown.

Now add the Venison and stir it around, breaking up the big lumps with the back of the spoon for 5 - 6 minutes until it has changed colour all over and is no longer lumpy. Stir in the tomato purée then the red wine. Bring to the boil and boil fast until all the liquid disappears.

Season with salt and pepper, the nutmeg and herbs and add 450ml game or beef stock. Bring to the boil, then simmer half covered for about 30 minutes (top up with more game or beef stock if it looks too dry).

After 30 minutes, stir in the milk, then simmer for a further 15 minutes until thick and creamy. Serve with freshly cooked spaghetti, sprinkled with basil leaves and freshly grated Parmesan cheese.

serves 6

2 tbsp. olive oil

75g cubed pancetta or streaky bacon

1 small onion, finely chopped

1 small carrot, finely chopped

1/2 stick celery, finely chopped

500g minced Verison

2 tbsp. tomato purée

200ml full-bodied red wine

1/4 tsp. freshly grated nutmeg

1 tsp. dried Herbes de Provence

450 - 600ml game or beef stock

100ml milk

450g dried spaghetti

fresh basil leaves and freshly grated Parmesan cheese,

to serve

salt and freshly ground black pepper

venison lasagne

A Venison lasagne is very simple to make and a great favourite with children. To get ahead, make the bolognese sauce the day before and the béchamel on the day – or just buy a reliable ready made white sauce. If you use fresh pasta it doesn't need pre-cooking, and is layered up just as it is. Make sure the Venison sauce is quite liquid. This will be absorbed into the pasta as it cooks.

Heat the olive oil in a saucepan and add the bacon. Cook for 2 - 3 minutes until browning. Add the onion, carrot and celery and brown these too.

Stir in the minced Venison and cook until just changing colour but not hardening, breaking it up with a wooden spoon. Pour in the milk, stir and boil hard to reduce. Add the tomato purée, wine and game or beef stock, mixing well. Season generously with salt, pepper and nutmeg. Bring to the boil, then lower the heat, cover and simmer for as long as you can – 2 hours if possible, or until the oil starts to separate on the surface.

Cook the sheets of dried lasagne in plenty of boiling water in batches according to manufacturer's instructions. Lift out with a slotted spoon and drain on a clean tea towel. Fresh pasta will not need cooking.

Heat the oven to 180C/350F/Gas Mark 4. Spoon one third of the Venison sauce into a buttered baking dish and spread out evenly. Cover this with four sheets of lasagne and spread with one third of the béchamel. Repeat twice more, finishing with a layer of béchamel covering the whole top. Sprinkle with Parmesan cheese. Bake in the oven for about 45 minutes until brown and bubbling.

Allow to stand for 10 minutes to settle and firm up a little before serving with a green salad.

serves 4 - 6

for the meat sauce:	3 tbsp. tomato purée
2 tbsp. olive oil	100ml dry white wine
75g pancetta or dry cured smoked bacon, diced	300ml game or beef stock
1 medium onion, finely chopped	freshly grated nutmeg
1 medium carrot, finely diced	about 12 sheets dried or fresh lasagne
1 stick of celery, finely chopped	900ml home or ready-made béchamel or white sauce
500g minced Venison	about 50g freshly grated Parmesan cheese
100ml milk	salt and freshly ground black pepper

venison and wild mushroom pies

These individual pies are easy to prepare in advance, you just pop them into the oven while you eat your starter. If you don't want to make pies, you can simply make the stew without the pastry, but serve with plenty of mash. Dried wild mushrooms are available in most supermarkets, but in season – pick your own, there's nothing better!

Soak the dried mushrooms in warm water for 30 minutes. Heat half the oil in a large casserole, add the onion, garlic, carrot and celery and cook for 5 - 10 minutes until softening. Stir in the pancetta and fry with the vegetables until just beginning to brown. Add the juniper berries, bay leaves and thyme, sprinkle in the flour, mix well, and set aside.

Heat the remaining olive oil in a large frying pan and fry the Venison quickly in batches on all sides until brown. Tip into the casserole as you go.

Deglaze the frying pan with the wine, bubble up and scrape up the sediment from the bottom of the pan. Pour over the Venison and vegetables.

Drain the mushrooms and add to the casserole with 150ml of the soaking water and the rowan jelly. Season really well, and give it a good stir. Add water to cover. Bring to the boil then cover and simmer for 1 1/2 hours until tender. Leave overnight to cool then refrigerate.

Next day, spoon the stew into six individual pie dishes.

Cut out six circles of pastry, a good 2.5cm wider than the dishes. Brush the edges of the dishes with beaten egg. Sit the pastry on top of the rim and press the pastry over the edge to seal tightly. Brush with more beaten egg, then make a couple of slits in the top. Set the pies on a couple of baking sheets and chill for 30 minutes or until ready to bake. Bake at 220C/425F/Gas Mark 7 for 20 - 25 minutes until the pastry is risen, crisp and golden brown.

serves 6	3 bay leaves
50g dried wild mushrooms	2 tbsp. chopped fresh thyme
6 tsp. olive oil	2 tbsp. plain white flour
1 onion, finely chopped	1kg diced Venison
3 garlic cloves, peeled and chopped	300ml dry red wine
1 large carrot, finely chopped	2 tbsp. rowan or redcurrant jelly
2 celery sticks, finely chopped	600g ready-rolled puff pastry
125g cubed pancetta, or streaky bacon	1 egg, beaten
8 juniper berries, crushed	salt and freshly ground black pepper

roast haunch of venison
with gooseberry and mint glaze

With no bones to cope with, this economical joint makes an ideal Sunday roast for all the family. It's delicious the following day sliced thinly and used in sandwiches.

Preheat the oven tc 230C/450F/Gas Mark 8.
Weigh the Venison and calculate the cooking time allowing 15 minutes per 450g for MEDIUM and 20 minutes for WELL DONE.

Rub the Venison with olive oil, salt and freshly ground black pepper. Put the Venison to brown in the oven for 15 minutes. Then turn down the heat to 200C/400F/GasMark 6.

Mix the gooseberry preserve with the mint sauce and brush all over the joint. Pour the red wine into the roasting pan. Roast in the oven for the remaining calculated time, basting once with more gooseberry preserve.

When cooked, take the Venison out of the oven. Lift the Venison onto a warm serving dish and cover loosely with foil. Leave to rest in a warm p ace for at least 20 minutes before carving.

Set the roasting pan over the heat, stir in the flour then cook for 2 - 3 minutes to brown the flour. Whisk in the consommé and port then bring to the boil and boil hard for 10 minutes to reduce by half. This will make quite a concentrated sauce. Taste and season, strain into a warm sauceboat and serve with the Venison.

Serve with a colourful medley of vegetables such as young carrots, French beans and broccoli and Hasselback Potatoes. (See page 41.)

serves 4 - 6

1 boned and rolled haunch roast of Venison (750g – 1kg)	150ml red wine
	1 tbsp. plain flour
olive oil or butter	410ml can beef consommé,
4 tbsp. gooseberry preserve, melted	or 400ml game or beef stock
1 tsp. mint sauce	300ml ruby or tawny port
	salt and freshly ground black pepper

roast haunch of venison
with rosemary and root vegetables

Try this for a Sunday roast instead of the usual joint. The sweetness of the earthy root vegetables complements the rosemary-scented Venison haunch. Ring the changes and use pumpkin or squash and even beetroot in the vegetable mixture.

Place the Venison in a non-metallic dish. Pierce the Venison trough the netting in twelve places with a small sharp knife.

Mix the olive oil, lemon zest and juice, chopped rosemary, salt and pepper together and pour over the Venison. Rub the marinade all over the haunch, cover and leave in a cool place to marinate for several hours or overnight.

The next day, preheat the oven to 230C/450F/Gas Mark 8.
Insert 12 small sprigs of fresh rosemary into the slits. Weigh the Venison and calculate the cooking time, allowing 15 minutes per 450g for MEDIUM Venison and 20 minutes for WELL DONE.

Scatter the carrots, parsnips, potatoes and onion with the remaining sprigs of rosemary over the base of a very large roasting pan. Lift the Venison out of the marinade and place on top of the vegetables. Pour over any remaining marinade.

Put into the oven for 15 minutes to seal and brown, then turn down the heat to 200C/400F/Gas Mark 6 and add 300ml game or beef stock. Roast for the calculated time, basting frequently with the juices in the pan.

When the Venison is cooked, transfer to a serving dish, cover loosely and allow to rest for 15 minutes in the cooled switched-off oven. This will make it easier to carve and re-distribute the juices throughout the Venison. Transfer the vegetables to a serving dish and keep warm. Carve the Venison into generous slices and serve with the vegetables.

serves 6

one boned and rolled haunch roast of Venison (750g - 1kg)	2 carrots, peeled and cut into large dice
3 tbsp. olive oil	2 parsnips, peeled and cut into large dice
grated zest and juice of 1 lemon	2 potatoes, peeled and cut into large dice
2 tbsp. chopped fresh rosemary plus 20 small sprigs of fresh rosemary	2 large mild onions, peeled and sliced
	300ml game or beef stock
	salt and freshly ground black pepper

pavé of venison
with real chips and béarnaise sauce

A beautiful Pavé of Venison (steak) cut from the haunch challenges the best beef fillet steak in both flavour and texture. It is best cooked RARE or MEDIUM RARE – overcooked Venison is a crime against nature! For speed, you can buy ready-made béarnaise sauce.

First make the chips. Heat the oil in a deep-fat fryer to 180°C. Whilst the oil is heating, cut the potatoes into long thick wedges. Add the chips to the hot oil and deep fry them for 12 - 15 minutes until the chips are a lovely golden colour. Lift the basket out of the oil and shake off any excess. Tip the chips into a dish lined with several sheets of kitchen paper and pat them dry. Keep warm in the oven with the door slightly ajar.

To make the béarnaise sauce. Put the vinegar, peppercorns, bay leaf, shallot, tarragon and chervil sprigs into a small saucepan and reduce over a medium heat to 1 tbsp. Remove from the heat to stop further evaporation.
In a small heatproof bowl, beat the egg yolks with a pinch of salt and 1 tsp. of the butter until slightly thickened. Strain in the reduction. Set the bowl snugly over a saucepan of simmering water and gradually whisk in the remaining butter piece by piece. The sauce will begin to thicken. Don't let the hot water touch the base of the bowl, or the sauce may curdle. When all the butter is added, stir in the chopped tarragon and chervil. Keep warm over a pan of warm water until ready to serve.

Heat a ridged griddle pan until smoking hot. Rub the Venison with a little olive oil and season with salt and pepper. Put the Venison on the hot griddle to sear for 2 - 3 minutes then turn the heat down to medium and cook without moving for another 2 - 3 minutes. Turn over and cook for a further 3 minutes. This is for RARE Venison – cook for 2 - 3 minutes longer for MEDIUM RARE. Lift onto a warm plate, cover loosely with foil and leave to rest in a warm place for 10 minutes to allow the Venison to relax. This will redistribute the juices through the Venison, giving it an even colour and keeping it juicy. Stir any collected juices into the sauce.

Serve the Pavé of Venison with the chips, béarnaise sauce and a mixed salad.

---

serves 2

450g Kerr's Pink or Maris Piper potatoes	1 sprig of fresh tarragon, plus 1 tsp. chopped
sunflower oil for deep frying	1 sprig of fresh chervil, plus 1 tsp. chopped
3 tbsp. white wine vinegar	2 egg yolks
6 black peppercorns	125g unsalted butter, cubed and softened
1 fresh bay leaf	two 150g Pavé (steaks) of Venison
1 shallot, finely chopped	salt and freshly ground black pepper

mango, green pepper and lime salsa for barbecued venison

This is a spicy fresh tasting salsa to serve with perfectly cooked Venison. Ideal for barbecues, and is best freshly made on the day.

Halve the mango by slicing off each side close to the stone. Peel off the skin with a potato peeler and cut the mango into small dice.

Mix with the onion, pepper, chilli and coriander. Mix the lime juice, zest and olive oil together and season with salt and pepper. Toss the salsa in the dressing and pile into a serving dish. Serve with barbecued Venison.

serves 4

1 large ripe mango

1/2 red onion, finely chopped

1 green pepper, halved seeded and finely diced

1/2 fresh red chilli, halved seeded and finely chopped

3 tbsp. chopped fresh coriander

finely grated zest and juice of 1 lime

2 - 3 tbsp. olive oil

salt and freshly ground black pepper

pavé of venison with blueberry and port sauce

A good sauce to rustle up at the last moment as it takes no time at all and can be made just as well with frozen blueberries as fresh.

First make the sauce. Put the sugar in a small saucepan, melt over a gentle heat then bring to the boil to caramelise. When a good golden colour, pour in the wine mixed with the vinegar. It will hiss and splutter. Stir over a gentle heat until any lumps are dissolved. Bring to the boil and boil fiercely until reduced by half.

Add the blueberries and simmer for 5 - 6 minutes until they are beginning to collapse and thicken the sauce. Remove from the heat, stir in the port and season with salt and pepper. Keep warm.

Heat a ridged griddle pan until smoking hot. Rub the Venison with olive oil and season with salt and freshly ground black pepper. Sear on the griddle for 2 - 3 minutes then turn the heat down to medium and cook without moving for another 2 - 3 minutes. Turn over and cook for a further 3 minutes for RARE. Cook for 2 - 3 minutes longer for MEDIUM RARE. Lift onto a plate, cover loosely with foil and leave to rest for 10 minutes.

Serve the Venison with the sauce, with some deep-fried sage leaves as a garnish.

serves 4

4 tbsp. sugar

1 tbsp. balsamic or sherry vinegar

150ml dry red wine

250g fresh or frozen blueberries

3 tbsp. ruby port

four 150g Pavé (steaks) of Venison

olive oil

deep-fried sage leaves, to garnish

salt and freshly ground black pepper

pavé of venison
with sun-dried tomato and basil butter

This thick cut is taken from the haunch and is the chef's favourite. It could almost be called the poor man's fillet. It has much more flavour and texture than fillet, cooks quickly, and is excellent value. Do not be tempted to overcook this – it will be tough but when cooked RARE or MEDIUM, the Venison remains tender and juicy. Pavé of Venison benefits from being rested for 10 minutes once cooked. If you haven't got a griddle pan a really heavy frying pan will do instead - you just won't have the griddle marks.

First make the savoury butter. Beat the butter until really soft, then beat in the remaining ingredients. Shape into a log and wrap in cling film. Chill for at least an hour until hard, or freeze.

Heat a ridged griddle pan until smoking hot. Rub the Venison with a little olive oil and season with salt and freshly ground black pepper. Put the Venison on the hot griddle to sear for 2 - 3 minutes then turn the heat down to MEDIUM and griddle without moving for another 2 - 3 minutes.

Turn over and cook for a further 3 minutes. This is for RARE – cook for 2 - 3 minutes longer for MEDIUM RARE. Transfer to a plate, cover loosely with foil and leave in a warm place close to the oven for 10 minutes to allow the Venison to relax, and the juices to redistribute through the meat.

Meanwhile, return the griddle to a medium heat and add 1 tbsp. olive oil. Add the tomatoes to the pan and cook for 3 - 4 minutes, shaking the pan occasionally, until they soften and begin to colour, but remain whole. Add a splash of balsamic vinegar and bubble for 1 minute.

Serve the steaks with the griddled tomatoes and their juices. Slice the butter thinly and put a couple of slices on top of each Pavé.

serves 2

for 200g Sun-dried Tomato and Basil Butter:	two 150g Pavé (steaks) of Venison
175g unsalted butter, softened	about 3 tbsp. olive oil
3 tbsp. finely shredded fresh basil	150g cherry tomatoes on the vine
6 sun-dried tomatoes in oil, drained and finely sliced	balsamic vinegar
2 tbsp. freshly grated Parmesan cheese	salt and freshly ground black pepper

pavé of venison
with red pepper and onion relish

This is a delicious sweet and sour relish that can be served hot or cold with rosy pink Venison steaks and some fluffy mash.

Heat the olive oil and add the onions and vinegar. Cook for 5 minutes until softening and beginning to brown.
Stir in the sliced peppers and cook gently for about 15 minutes until the vegetables are completely soft. Season with salt and pepper and stir in the chopped thyme. Keep warm.

Place a large heavy frying pan on a high heat. Rub the Venison with olive oil and season with salt and freshly ground black pepper. Sear the Venison in the pan for 2 - 3 minutes then turn the heat down to medium and cook without moving for another 2 - 3 minutes. Turn over and cook for a further 3 minutes for RARE. Cook for 2 - 3 minutes longer for MEDIUM RARE. Lift onto a plate, cover loosely with foil and leave to rest for 10 minutes, this will redistribute the juices into the Venison, giving an even colour and keeping it juicy.

Serve with the pepper and onion relish.

serves 4	2 large red peppers, halved, seeded and finely sliced
for the Red Pepper and Onion Relish:	2 tsp. chopped fresh thyme
2 tbsp. olive oil	four 150g Pavé (steaks) of Venison
2 medium onions, halved and thinly sliced	olive oil
1 tbsp. cider vinegar	salt and freshly ground black pepper

medallions of venison with melting onions

Miles better than a ready meal, and almost as quick – this is the answer to a fast and easy additive-free meal when you get in from work. The cream is an optional extra!

Take a large frying pan and heat the oil over a medium heat. Add the onions, stir and turn down the heat, then allow the onions to soften and go translucent for about 15 minutes. (While they cook you can make some mashed potato).

Turn the heat up to medium, push the onions to one side and add the medallions. Cook, occasionally turning the medallions, for 6 - 8 minutes until the Venison is browned and beginning to firm up. Add the cream (if using) and parsley to the pan, stirring into the onions. Bring up to the boil, taste and check the seasoning.

Delicious with mustard mash, buttered fresh green beans and garden peas.

serves 2

for the melting onions:

3 tbsp. olive oil

2 large onions, about 250g, thinly sliced

2 tbsp. chopped fresh parsley or thyme

4 tbsp. double cream or creme fraîche (optional)

6 Medallions of Venison, approx 300g

salt and freshly ground black pepper

cooking a perfect fillet of venison

This is THE perfect, no-fuss dinner party dish. The Venison is tender and juicy and easy to slice. It only takes 20 - 30 minutes in the oven to cook and can be browned well before-hand, cooled and refrigerated until 10 minutes before you want to cook it. Bring the Venison to room temperature for 10 minutes before popping it in the oven. The crunchy golden potatoes were invented by the Hasselbacken Restaurant in Stockholm, Sweden and are an excellent alternative to roast potatoes.

Preheat the oven to 200C/400F/Gas Mark 6. Rub the fillet all over with the olive oil, then season with salt and freshly ground black pepper. For a very neat presentation, tie the Venison up along its length at 4cm intervals with fine string. This will firm it up and give it a good round shape.

Place a peeled potato in the bowl of a wooden spoon and make vertical slices, 2 - 3mm apart, about 3/4 of the way through each potato. The wooden spoon will stop the knife cutting all the way through. Place the potatoes in a buttered baking dish, cuts uppermost. Melt half of the butter and pour it over the potatoes, then sprinkle with salt.

Heat a heavy roasting pan or very large frying pan until very hot indeed and add the fillet. Brown this quickly and evenly all the way round. Season again and place the Venison and potatoes in the oven. Roast the Venison for 20 minutes for RARE or 25 - 30 minutes for MEDIUM. Bake the potatoes for 30 minutes, now and then basting the with melted butter. After 30 minutes, sprinkle the breadcrumbs and grated cheese (optional) over the potatoes.

When the Venison is cooked to your liking, remove it from the oven and transfer to a warm serving plate to relax for about 10 minutes. While you make a gravy, finish cooking the potatoes for another 15 minutes until golden and crisp.

Put the roasting pan over the heat, sprinkle with a tbsp. of flour and cook for a minute until brown. Deglaze the pan with a glass of red wine or port, scraping up the bits sticking to the bottom of the pan (at this stage you could add a couple of dried mushrooms for extra flavour). Whisk in the game or beef stock, season well and bring to the boil. Simmer for 10 minutes until syrupy. Strain into a gravy boat.

Slice the Venison and lay on a bed of thinly shredded radicchio, and serve with the wine gravy and Hasselback potatoes.

---

serves 6 - 8

1kg Venison fillet, at room temperature	12 medium-sized potatoes, peeled
2 tbsp. olive oil	3 tbsp. melted butter
1 glass of red wine or port	1 - 2 tbsp. dried breadcrumbs
300ml game or beef stock	3 tbsp. freshly grated Parmesan cheese (optional)
For the Hasselback Potatoes:	salt and freshly ground black pepper

roast french rack of venison
with garlic, rosemary and mustard crust

French Racks of Venison make entertaining both easy and spectacular. They are so quick to cook, and easily carved into cutlets to serve. If you have time, you can clean the bones thoroughly before cooking by scraping with a small sharp knife for a truly professional finish.

Preheat the oven to 200°C/400°F/Gas Mark 6. With a very sharp knife, score the outer meaty surface of the Venison very lightly in a criss-cross manner, to hold the herb crust. Season the rack of Venison generously with salt and freshly ground black pepper.

Mix the mustard, softened butter and garlic to form a paste. Mix in the breadcrumbs, chopped parsley and rosemary. Press this over the scored meaty side of the Venison and place on a baking tray.

Roast the Venison for about 20 minutes for RARE Venison or about 25 minutes for MEDIUM Venison. After roasting, remove from the oven and leave to rest in a warm place for 10 minutes before carving between the bones into cutlets. Serve with new potatoes, baby tomatoes roasted in olive oil and some buttered leeks.

serves 3 – 4

1 French Rack of Venison (7 - 9 bones)

for the garlic, rosemary and mustard crust:

2 tbsp. Dijon mustard

3 tbsp. butter, softened

3 garlic cloves, finely chopped

8 tbsp. fresh white breadcrumbs

6 tbsp. finely chopped fresh parsley

3 tbsp. finely chopped fresh rosemary

salt and freshly ground black pepper

crown roast of venison
with celery and lemon thyme skirlie

This impressive dish is easy to make with a well-trimmed Rack of Venison. Cook two for a spectacular dinner party dish for eight. Skirlie could almost be called Scottish couscous – deliciously simple toasted oatmeal with onion, lemon thyme and celery. No potatoes necessary.

Preheat the oven to 200C/400F/Gas Mark 6.
For a really professional finish, scrape each bone clean of any Venison or gristle. Bend the rack into a circle, with the trimmed side of the ribs inside (bones curving outwards). With a sharp knife, nick through the sinew between each cutlet to help the rack bend into shape. Join the two ends together with the help of a couple wooden cocktail sticks or a stitch or two using fine kitchen string and a heavy darning needle.

Melt the butter in a roasting pan until foaming, add the thyme sprigs and place the Venison on top. Wrap up the end of the bones with kitchen foil to prevent them from burning and brush the roast with melted butter. Roast for about 20 minutes for RARE Venison or 25 minutes for MEDIUM RARE Venison, basting once.

While the Venisnon is cooking, heat the oil, fat or dripping in a frying pan and add the onion and celery. Cook over a gentle heat for 5 minutes until just beginning to turn golden. Stir in the oatmeal and "skirl" (stir) around the pan for a couple of minutes until the fat is absorbed and the oatmeal smells warm and toasted. Stir in the thyme and season well. Keep warm.

When the Venison is cooked, remove it from the oven and leave to rest while you make the gravy.

Pour off all but a tbsp. of butter from the roasting taking care not to pour away any of the meat juices. Stir in the flour, scraping any sticky sediment from the bottom of the pan. Add the game or beef stock and stir until boiling. Simmer for 2 minutes. Taste, season and strain into a gravy boat. Remove the foil from the bones. Garnish with fresh thyme in the centre, surround with the Skirlie and serve the gravy separately.

---

serves 3 - 4

1 French Rack of Venison (7 - 9 bones)	50ml olive oil, bacon fat, or beef dripping
sprigs of fresh thyme, plus extra to garnish	1 medium onion, finely chopped
4 tbsp. melted butter	2 celery sticks, finely chopped
1 tbsp. plain white flour	125g medium or coarse oatmeal
300ml good game or beef stock	2 tbsp. chopped fresh lemon thyme
for the celery and lemon skirlie:	salt and freshly ground black pepper

venison stroganoff

The secret of a perfect Venison Stroganoff is the speed at which the Venison strips are cooked. It must be quickly cooked in a very hot pan to seal in the juices or the meat will stew in its own juices and become grey and tough. This is a very quick supper dish – add a spoonful of grain mustard if you like.

Melt half the butter in a frying pan, add the onion and gently cook until soft. Add the mushrooms and toss over a high heat for 30 seconds. Add the wine and the game or beef stock. Boil rapidly to reduce the liquid to about 4 tbsp. Stir well and tip into a bowl.

Now heat the oil anc the remaining butter in the empty pan. Drop in the Venison strips and stir-fry over a high heat until browned on the outside, but still pink inside.

Turn the heat down and pour in the brandy and ignite. As soon as the flames have died down return the mushroom mixture to the pan. Stir in the cream, bring to the boil. Taste and season. (If the sauce is too thin remove the Venison and boil the sauce rapidly to reduce it). Serve with boiled rice, and a good sprinkling of parsley.

serves 4

50g butter	150ml good game or beef stock
500g stir-fry Venison	1 tbsp. olive oil
1 medium onion, sliced finely	3 tbsp. brandy
300g brown-cap mushrooms, quartered	200ml crème fraîche
150ml dry white wine	boiled rice, to serve
	salt and freshly ground black pepper

venison tagine

This makes an exotic change from the humble stew, especially when served with couscous. It is always better eaten the next day to allow the flavours to develop. It freezes well.

Place the Venison in a large saucepan together with the onion and garlic. Fry for about 10 minutes, stirring frequently. (This is the authentic method used in North Africa. The meat will gently stew in its own juices, keeping very moist and tender).

Add the bay leaves, paprika, cumin, fennel seeds and tomato purée, mixing well. Pour in the game or beef stock and season very well with salt and freshly ground black pepper. Bring to the boil, lower the heat, cover the pan and simmer for 45 minutes to 1 hour or until the Venison is tender.

Meanwhile, put the olives into a small pan and top up with cold water. Bring to the boil then simmer for 5 - 7 minutes then remove and drain (this will remove any bitterness).

When the Venison is tender, add the olives and tomatoes, stir well and simmer for a few minutes. Mix the flour with a little water and stir into the stew with half the coriander. Cook for a further minute or two - until the sauce is thickened.
Serve sprinkled with the remaining coriander and a big bowl of steaming couscous.

serves 4 - 6

1kg diced Venison	1 tsp. crushed fennel seeds
30g butter	3 tbsp. tomato purée
4 tbsp. olive oil	1.3 litres game or beef stock
2 large onions, roughly chopped	4 medium ripe tomatoes, quartered or halved
3 garlic cloves, crushed	250g good black olives, stoned
3 bay leaves	1 tbsp. plain white flour
1 tbsp. sweet paprika	4 tbsp. finely chopped coriander or parsley
1 tsp. ground cumin	couscous, to serve
	salt and freshly ground black pepper

thai green curry with venison

Venison marries well with the strong flavours in this Thai curry. Some commercial Thai curry pastes are very hot so add less at the beginning – you can always add more. Serve with Thai jasmine rice.

Heat the oil in a large sauté pan or wok until smoking and add the sliced onion and red pepper. Cook over a high heat until the onions are just beginning to catch and go brown around the edges.

Stir in the curry paste, cook for 1 minute, then pour in the coconut milk, game or beef stock and lime leaves or zest. Bring to the boil then turn down the heat and simmer gently for 10 minutes.

Add the peas or broccoli and simmer for 2 minutes, then add the baby sweet corn and simmer for a further 5 minutes or until the vegetables are tender and the sauce slightly thickened.

Drop the stir-fry Venison into the curry and simmer for 2 - 3 minutes.

Serve the curry in warmed deep soup bowls with boiled Thai Jasmine rice and extra coriander.

---

serves 4 - 6

3 tbsp. sunflower oil

1 onion, finely chopped

1 red pepper, halved, seeded and sliced

1 yellow pepper, halved seeded and sliced

4 - 6 tbsp. Thai green curry paste

2 x 400ml cans coconut milk

3 kaffir lime leaves (or grated zest of 1 lime)

250g frozen peas or small broccoli florets

100g whole baby sweet corn

2 tbsp. chopped fresh coriander

500g stir-fry Venison

salt and freshly ground black pepper

carbonnade of venison

Fine collops of lean Venison are slowly braised with caramelised onions and beer in this classic recipe. The dish takes its name from the time when it was simmered over a charcoal braise or charbon, hence the name carbonnade. The beer mellows into the sweet onions and makes a subtle rich gravy. For a darker stew, use half light ale and half stout.

Preheat the oven to 150°C/300°F/Gas Mark 2. Cut each medallion horizontally into two chunky pieces.

Heat the oil in a large heavy-based frying pan and brown the Venison in batches over a high heat. Transfer to a large casserole, using a slotted spoon.

Add the onions to the oil and the remaining juices in the pan and cook for 10 minutes, stirring until they begin to soften. Add the garlic and sugar, mix well and cook gently for 10 minutes or until they begin to brown and caramelise. Stir in the flour, then gradually stir in the beer. Bring to the boil, scraping up any sediment from the bottom of the pan, then pour over the browned Venison in the casserole.

Pour the game or beef stock over the Venison and onions and add the herbs and plenty of pepper. Stir lightly to mix. Bring to a simmer, then cover tightly and cook in the oven for about 45 minutes.

When cooked, carefully stir in the vinegar and cook for a further 30 minutes or until the Venison is very tender indeed. Check the seasoning. Serve garnished with chopped parsley, accompanied by boiled potatoes and some crunchy Savoy cabbage.

---

serves 6

900g Medallions of Venison

2 tbsp. olive oil

700g onions, halved and thinly sliced

4 garlic cloves, crushed

2 tbsp. light brown sugar

3 tbsp. flour

600ml pale ale or lager

300ml game or beef stock

1 fresh bay leaf

2 large fresh thyme sprigs

30ml wine or cider vinegar

chopped parsley, to garnish

salt and freshly ground black pepper

venison goulash

A rich and filling stew for cold autumn and winter nights and easy to make in quantity for entertaining large numbers. Serve it with soured cream or Greek yogurt and plenty of chopped fresh chives for a fresh oniony tang. If you prefer a smoky taste, use a mixture of pimentón or Spanish smoked paprika and sweet paprika.

Preheat the oven to 160C/325F/Gas Mark 3.

Heat the oil in a large casserole and brown the Venison all over. Remove the Venison to a plate then add the onion and garlic to the casserole. Cook over a medium heat for about 15 minutes until the onion is just tinged with brown.

Mix the paprika with the flour, thyme and juniper berries. Tip the Venison and any juices back into the casserole, add the flour and paprika mixture, stir well and cook for a couple of minutes.
Pour in the passata and add the game or beef stock, season well, stir and bring to the boil. Turn down the heat, cover with a lid and simmer in the oven for about 1 1/2 hours.

20 minutes before it is ready, add the potatoes, replace the lid and cook for 20 minutes. Drizzle with sour cream and sprinkle with chopped chives. Serve with baked potatoes or noodles.

serves 6 - 8

1kg diced Venison

2 tbsp. vegetable oil

2 garlic cloves, chopped

2 tbsp. plain flour

2 tbsp. sweet paprika

6 juniper berries, crushed

2 tsp. dried thyme

400ml Italian passata (strained sieved tomatoes)

200ml game or beef stock

600g potatoes, peeled and cut into large chunks

soured cream or Greek yogurt and chopped

fresh chives to garnish

salt and freshly ground black pepper

cooking a perfect pavé of venison

This is one of the best ways to cook a Pavé (steak). Quickly searing the Venison in the pan forms a tasty crust on the outside of the meat and seals in the juices. Finishing the cooking in the oven ensures even cooking throughout. Once cooked, transfer the steaks to a warm plate to relax the fibres and redistribute the juices throughout the Venison, giving it an even colour. You must remove the Venison from the hot pan to ensure that it doesn't go on cooking and become tough.

Preheat oven to 200C/400F/Gas Mark 6.

Heat an ovenproof heavy frying pan until smoking hot. Rub the Venison with a little olive oil, and season with salt and freshly ground black pepper. Put the Venison into the hot frying pan, turn the heat down to medium, and sear for 2 - 3 minutes (do not be tempted to move it around or the outside crust will be spoiled).

Turn over and sear on the other side for 2 - 3 minutes. Place the pan in the oven and cook for 6 minutes RARE or 8 minutes MEDIUM RARE.

When cooked, remove the Venison from the oven, transfer onto a warm plate, cover loosely with foil and leave to rest for 10 minutes.

To make a sauce, add a good splash of red wine to the empty frying pan, bring to the boil, scraping up the sticky sediment from the bottom of the pan, and boil until reduced and syrupy. Taste and season.

Serve the Pavés drizzled with a little olive oil, a huge mixed salad, and some boiled new potatoes or vegetable crisps.

---

serves 4
four 150g Pavé (steaks) of Venison

olive oil
salt and freshly ground black pepper

cooking venison medallions

Venison medallions are the answer to the "what will we have for supper tonight?" question. They are cooked in minutes, tender and juicy and only need a selection of simply cooked fresh vegetables or an interesting salad to complete the meal.

Season the medallions with salt and pepper. Heat a heavy frying pan over a medium heat. Add the olive oil, wait until it heats up then add the medallions. They should instantly sizzle. Cook over a steady heat for 2 - 3 minutes. Do not move them. Turn over and cook on the second side and cook for a further 2 - 3 minutes.

The Venison should be pink and in no way overcooked. Remove to a warm plate and leave to rest for 5 minutes before serving.

Delicious with mashed or boiled potatoes and a pile of buttered mange tout.

serves 2

6 Medallions of Venison, approximately 300g

1 tbsp. olive oil

salt and freshly ground black pepper

venison and red pepper casserole

This could easily become a family favourite. A simple stew made more interesting by the addition of red peppers. If you don't like red peppers, use sliced carrot, parsnip or even pumpkin or squash instead. You needn't use wine for an everyday dish - substitute stock with a dash of red wine vinegar to give it depth. Add a blob of crème fraîche for a richer sauce.

Pat the Venison dry with kitchen paper and toss with the flour. Heat the olive oil in a casserole and quickly brown the Venison all over.

Add the onions, garlic, celery and peppers and cook for a few minutes until golden and starting to soften.
Pour in the game or beef stock, red wine and bay leaf and stir well. Season with salt and pepper. Bring to the boil, cover then simmer gently for about 2 hours or until the Venison is tender. Top up with extra game or beef stock or water as necessary.

Serve with mash, noodles or pasta and steamed broccoli and courgettes.

serves 4	2 celery sticks, diced
500g diced Venison	2 red peppers, halved, seeded and sliced
3 tbsp. plain white flour	300ml game or beef stock
2 tbsp. olive oil	300ml dry red wine
2 onions, sliced	1 bay leaf
1 garlic clove, crushed	salt and freshly ground black pepper

partridge breasts
with orange, honey and sesame seeds

A very quick starter and one of Ingela's star dishes. It can be rustled up in moments and is very impressive. The longer you marinate them the better, but they will still taste fine with only 10 minutes in the marinade. Serve on a bed of pretty salad leaves.

First prepare the marinade. Mix the orange zest with the honey, olive oil and vinegar. Add the partridge breasts, mix well cover and leave to marinate in the fridge for up to 2 hours.

Remove the breasts from the marinade and heat a frying pan until quite hot. Add the breasts and brown quickly for 1 minute on each side. Add the marinade, seasoning and the sesame seeds and bring to the boil. Simmer until the sauce is syrupy and begins to caramelise slightly.

Remove from the heat and pile 3 breasts onto each of four plates lined with salad leaves. Drizzle with the sauce and serve immediately.

serves 4

12 prepared skinless partridge breasts

finely grated zest and juice of 1 orange

2 tbsp. runny honey

4 tbsp. olive oil

2 tsp. balsamic vinegar

2 tsp. sesame seeds

young salad leaves, to serve

salt and freshly ground black pepper

pheasant breasts with sherry and pine nuts

This recipe is based on a dish of quail I tasted in southern Spain. Sherry and pheasant were made for each other, especially if you use slightly "salty" manzanilla. Saffron adds an exotic fragrance and beautiful golden colour.

Season the breasts with salt and freshly ground black pepper and wrap each with 2 slices of pancetta or bacon. Heat a frying pan and add the breasts to the pan. Cook quickly until brown all over then remove to a plate.

Add the onion and garlic and cook gently until golden. Stir in the saffron, pine nuts and sherry, then add the pheasant breasts and any juices collected on the plate.

Bring to the boil then half-cover and simmer very gently for 8 - 10 minutes until cooked through, turning the breasts once. Taste the sauce - adjust the seasoning and stir in the parsley. Serve with crumbly sautée potatoes or more indulgent creamy Dauphinoise Potatoes and a selection of roasted Mediterranean vegetables.

serves 4

4 prepared skinless pheasant breasts

8 slices pancetta or thinly sliced dry-cure streaky bacon

1 large onion, finely chopped

2 garlic cloves, finely chopped

a pinch of saffron threads

2 - 3 tbsp. pine nuts, toasted

200ml dry sherry

2 tbsp. chopped fresh parsley or coriander

salt and freshly ground black pepper

savoury butters and marinades

Savoury butters are very handy to have in the fridge or freezer to slice and melt on top of grilled, pan-fried or barbecued Venison. As the butter melts, it releases the flavours within.

Chilli, Lime and Black Pepper Butter serves 6 - 8.
Beat 175g softened unsalted butter until really soft, then beat in 2 fresh chopped red chillies, 3 tbsp. sweet chilli sauce, the finely grated zest of 1 lime, a sqeeze of lime juice, 3 tbsp. chopped fresh coriander (optional), a little salt and 1 tsp. crushed black peppercorns. Shape into a log and wrap in cling film. Chill for at least an hour until hard, or freeze. Slice thinly into discs and serve on top of grilled or barbecued Venison. (Will freeze for up to 3 months.)

Juniper and Ginger Butter serves 6 - 8.
Beat 175g softened unsalted butter until really soft, then beat in 3 crushed and finely chopped juniper berries, 1 tbsp. finely chopped fresh ginger, 1 tbsp. finely chopped stem ginger, 1 tbsp. gin, salt and freshly ground black pepper to taste. Shape into a log and wrap in cling film. Chill for at least an hour until hard, or freeze. Slice thinly into discs and serve on top of grilled or barbecued Venison. (Will freeze for up to 3 months.)

Basil and Sun-dried Tomato and Basil Butter (See page 35.)

Marinades are used to further tenderise Venison, add extra flavour and lock in the moisture. The basic marinade is best for pan-fried, grilled or barbecued cuts of Venison. The cooked marinade is particularly packed with flavour and best for larger cuts, diced Venison or joints that will be braised or cooked in liquid.

Basic Marinade for Venison Enough for 1kg.
Mix 100ml extra virgin olive oil, 3 tbsp. wine vinegar or lemon or lime juice, 2 finely chopped garlic cloves, 2 tbsp. chopped fresh thyme or sage or 1 tbsp. dried sage, 2 crushed juniper berries, 1 bay leaf and 1 tsp. freshly ground black pepper together (with no salt at this stage) and pour into a large strong plastic bag. Add the Venison and seal the bag. Shake it a couple of times to mix the marinade with the Venison. Leave to marinate in a cool place for 2 - 4 hours or longer. Strain off the marinade and pat the Venison dry with kitchen paper when ready to cook. Reserve the marinade and use to baste whole cuts of Venison, seasoning with salt last of all.

Basic Cooked Marinade for Braising Venison Enough for 1.5kg.
Heat 100ml olive oil and add 2 sliced carrots, 2 sliced celery sticks, 2 quartered onions and 2 chopped garlic cloves. Cook over a medium heat until beginning to soften and brown. Add 2 tbsp. mixed chopped fresh rosemary and thyme, 2 cloves, 3 crushed juniper berries, 1 bay leaf, 1 bottle dry white wine, 2 tbsp. balsamic vinegar and 1 tsp. crushed black peppercorns. Bring to the boil, cover and simmer for 30 minutes. Remove from the heat, cool completely then use to marinate the Venison as above. Use the strained marinade as the braising liquid for Venison, adding more fresh vegetables as needed.

sourcing and nutrition

Highland Game Scotland

Highland Game promotes and processes Wild Venison from the heart of the Scottish Highlands, supplying Wholesalers, Caterers, Multiple Retailers and Direct On-Line Sales throughout the UK with Quality Assured Scottish Wild Venison, securing prime quality from 'hill to table'.

Nutrition

Scottish Wild Venison is low in cholesterol and saturated fat but high in essential minerals and protein. It also offers a rich source of vitamin B complex. Venison is pure and natural, completely free from salt and other additives – it is truly organic as only wild produce can be.

highland game venison product specifications

Haunch Roast of Venison: Netted haunch roast, cut from the knuckle end.

500g / 1kg Fillet of Venison: A hand finished piece, cut from the thick end of the fillet.

French Rack of Venison: 9 bone, French cut, hand-trimmed rack.

Pavé of Venison: A 150g thick-cut steak, a French cut from one of the top 3 muscles of the haunch.

Medallions of Venison: A 50g (approximately 1.25cm thick) collop-style medallion - ideal for quick cooking.

Diced Venison: Hand-diced, 2.5cm cubes from specially selected cuts of Venison.

Venison Stir Fry: Long hand-cut strips of Venison from specially selected cuts - ideal for quick cooking.

Mince: Finest quality lean mince - makes the best bolognaise sauce ever.

Burgers: 125g lean burger, made from choice Venison cuts and specially seasoned - a healthy burger option.

Sausages: Hand finished in a natural casing using traditional ingredients.

Game Birds used in this book

Pheasant Breasts: Skinned trimmed fillets, wing bone removed.

Partridge Breasts: Skinless trimmed fillets, wing bone removed.

notes:

notes:

Put Scottish Wild Venison at the top of your shopping list!

This delicious and tender meat can be prepared as easily as top quality beef but is much lower in saturated fat and cholesterol. Wild Venison is highly nutritious and rich in protein which makes it an important ingredient of a healthy modern diet.

In the past, prime quality wild Venison was difficult to find outside specialist game dealers and restaurants. Highland Game expertly sources and prepares a choice of the best ready-to-cook cuts. We offer a UK next day delivery service of game boxes ranging from succulent Venison burgers to tender fillet of Venison.

Highland Game's accreditation to the Scottish Quality Wild Venison assurance scheme ensures that our rigorous quality and traceability methods meet only the highest standards, and has earned us several prestigious awards.

Our Venison is sourced from the heart of the Scottish Highlands where the deer roam and graze freely in their natural habitat.

Not only is this natural meat easy to cook, but its flavour and tenderness will make it an instant hit with friends and family. Whether you are cooking Venison Lasagne for your family or a French Rack of Venison for your dinner party guests, this cook book is an inspiration for everyday and seasonal cooking.

Wild Venison is a versatile and healthy alternative to traditional meats. There is nothing added – nothing taken away. It is just pure and natural.

Shop on-line and enjoy our special seasonal offers.

Order a Highland Game Box today.

Christian Nissen, Managing Director

Highland Game
SCOTLAND
PURVEYORS OF FINE FOODS

www.highlandgame.com
Highland Game, Dryburgh Industrial Estate, Baird Avenue, Dundee DD2 3TN